The Long Night

of Flying

The Long Night
of Flying

Poems

Sharon Olson

Sixteen Rivers Press SAN FRANCISCO

Published by Sixteen Rivers Press
P.O. Box 640663
San Francisco, California 94164-0663
www.sixteenrivers.org

ISBN-13: 978-0-9767642-1-2
ISBN-10: 0-9767642-1-0
Library of Congress Control Number 2005908549

Cover Art: *Coast Scene with Figures (Beverly Shore)*, 1869, by John Frederick Kensett, oil on canvas, reprinted with permission of the Wadsworth Atheneum Museum of Art, Hartford, CT. The Ella Gallup Sumner and Mary Catlin Sumner Collection Fund.

Acknowledgments

Grateful acknowledgment is made to the following publications, in which poems in this collection previously appeared:

American Literary Review ("The Unthinkable"); *The Crab Orchard Review* ("Madrileño"); *Convolvulus* ("Afternoon in Pienza" and "San Michele"); *disquietingmuses* ("Untitled" and "Remembering in Part"); *Fire in the Hills* ("Berkeley-Oakland Hills, October 1991"); *Kalliope* ("The Two Women"); *Peace or Perish* ("On the Way to the Bomb Shelter"); *The Sand Hill Review* ("At Fourteen, Knowing Nothing" and "Resting After the Fall"); *Santa Clara Review* ("Bouilland," "Lucia," and "Sex Is the Mathematics Urge Sublimated"); *The Seattle Review* ("The Village of the Mermaids"); *The Worcester Review* ("Concord").

A number of poems in this collection appeared first in the chapbook *Clouds Brushed in Later* (San Jose Poetry Center Press, 1987).

I would like to express my deepest thanks to the members of Sixteen Rivers Press, the Tuesday Night poets, my friend Marilyn Green, who was there from the beginning, and my companion of many journeys, Bill.

For my brother Bruce, 1932–53,
whose yellow Piper Cub was never found

Contents

A Chorus of Pines

Listening for Beauty

Shattering the Surface of Afternoon

The Long Night of Flying

what would the world be
were it not filled with
the incessant bustling of the poet
among the birds and stones

ZBIGNIEW HERBERT
from "A Tale"

A Chorus of Pines

Fellini Remembers His Childhood

Father, we have come to take you
on this fresh October day to the country,
where the leaves are the color of old books
and as frail as you, turning,
always turning in the mind.
We sit on blankets near the family farm
and try to draw you near us
with bread and cheese and brave smiles—
nothing that you want.

And so you leave us to climb the old elm,
making your way to a level branch
where you are at last comfortable
and can begin shouting, *Voglio una donna*,
I want a woman! you say, you keep saying.
Your thin legs wrap around smooth bark,
and you listen for the sound
of skirts rustling among the leaves,
wanting the woman you remember,
or many women who have become one woman,
who crosses the fields slowly
and pulls herself up into the tree,
a woman whose body brings to you
garlic and olive oil, *baccalà*
simmering on a low fire.

When the wind dies and the sun
squints at you through the branches,

you remember the end of the story:
the woman never comes, not today or any day.
Your legs dangle and your arms reach down,
a signal you want to be taken home.

Verdi Goes for a Walk with Giuseppina

Just for one moment, Giuseppina, do not think of the children,
stretch your legs as far as they will go,
the way you stretch them in bed after morning's pleasure.
I want to show you the lily beds,
and the shepherd watching us from the trees
his ears are made of rough stone, he is frozen by the pond.
There is so much to show you, you must take off your gloves.
Beside the path are lupine and buttercups,
remember to bite into the base of the clover.
The road to Busseto is lined with such treasures, and oh,
Giuseppina, the pink lilies are pushing up their tender heads,
long stems exploding into ribbons and bows,
waving at us in the shadow of the elm.
At the base of your ear I will bite the sweet clover
until you rise up swaying and dreaming,
ours is the lily bed stretching and pulling.
We should be married, Giuseppina,
I know I have promised you.
I am not practical, Giuseppina,
you should take me now,
this rare moment when I am not hearing music,
this very moment when my head is drowning in lilies.

Bouilland

1.

The wind in the pines begins to speak
like a chorus waiting offstage, its song
amplified by a hidden microphone.

2.

At daybreak the clouds soar like segmented
spinal columns, each section proclaiming:
we can bend, we can bend.

3.

Marguerite rises with the sun,
dips her face into a blue-striped bowl of water,
creates one and then two waist-long braids,
and practices the speech she gives daily
in her slowest, most precise French,
to American ladies and occasional young men, walking:
Tout droit au bout de la rue—
the way she knows to the Abbaye Ste-Marguerite
(yes, it is her name)—
white skeletal ribs of stone
rising from moss and blackberry vine,
and between the arches, pockets of sky
resting on green hillsides of clay.

4.

One day, she will walk there with an occasional young man,
her moist skin taking in, like fine clay,
the pressure of his fingers on her arm.
She cannot have enough of this moment
that leaves her without words,
deafened by the full chorus of pines.

Spinning

I am bicycling past you
in my gray tweed hat and coat
and long white skirt,
my nose at a familiar slant—
It's Virginia, you say.

It's late and I must visit
St. George's Gardens, a green
glen where the gravestones
are propped up against the wall,
a great weight lifted from the dead.

We are not dead yet, my dear,
but we know what it's like to be
fatherless daughters, grown women
leading ourselves by the hand.
We only seem to be empty,

like the black pools that line
the path in St. George's, this place
that is not quite a cemetery,
where my bicycle spins along beside me
and rain washes the earth in brown silk.

When we have learned how to make
decisions again, and our eyes are
washed and clear, we will sit
at a table and discuss the goodness
of wine, the manliness of daughters.

Bride of the Wind

Everything is possible in Granada.
Horses gallop on the tips of his fingers
as he slaps the flanks of his guitar
faster and then not faster, hooves clicking,
riding dark paths in search
of the woman he has met tonight,
who speaks to him but has revealed nothing,
an agreement they whisper hurriedly, eyes flashing.
Tell me the story, she says, of the sad horse,
how she stumbles over the quivering
strings you hold in your fingers,
how you want to steady her,
wipe the sweat from the curve of her back.
And when her mind races, he says,
I reach over like this
and place my hand in her hair.

For Bill Fite, Wherever You Are

I would recognize you even now,
of all the boys
you were the only perfect dancer.
In response to my supple smile
you wrote your name
as many times as you dared—
for the first dance, and the third,
and the fifth, and the eighth.

As the lesson winds down, Miss Gollatz
signals us to lead the grand promenade,
the final march down long, carpeted stairs
to the lobby where the boys
are to help us with our coats.
Only you kept hold of my arm,
led me into the warm Pasadena night
where the smog had left us
this strange indigo sky,
and electricity
kept the horizon light.

Moving from Stone to Stone

The train reached Parma, and I arrived
as if by bicycle, still spinning, on a dusty road.

This was my first journey alone, I was eighteen,
and impressions of a previous life suddenly appeared,
something about the way shadows fell on stone.

It was only a movie I had seen, figures pressing
close as they walked along the riverbank,
water sliding away from them as they spoke.

The movie flickered in black and white, but
this was the color of biscuits, yellow walls,
red roofs baking in the sun.

The museum had closed for the day,
and the inside of the Duomo held no one
but the sacristan, whose dark skirts I followed
up the stairs to the very edge of the world.

Above me the *Assumption of the Virgin*,
Correggio, 1522, on the inside of the dome.

This story is not the usual Italian one
of compromise. No words reached my ears—
a kiss, *signorina*, please just a kiss.

As the lights came on, angels ran in circles
as if waiting for a future life,
knowing just how it will take place.

View from the Back

The man I am looking at is thinking.
Rodin has covered his back with scars.
I see him from the door of the museum
like a man surprised in my bathroom,
someone I hardly know, or my father,
or brother, so deep in thought
he does not feel my eyes staring,
and I tell myself to stand still
as long as his privacy enfolds him.
And you wonder why I don't tell you
the Cézannes I have seen are lovely.
What is lovelier is this man I have
stumbled across in the doorway, whose
scars lie open to the public eye,
who feels the sharp wind rising
from the bay, whose bathrobe lies
on the floor in blue folds, whose
mind will be empty the moment
he rises to leave.

Naming the Dead

We have entered the port illegally. We thought we were in a historic district. The belltower is inaccessible—vertigo conveniently postponed. History is for sale in Benicia. Unisys, one of the first customers, has traded up for an old Colonial. A designing woman in stirrup pants grazes the treasure mart where real artifacts, sprayed gold, are for sale.

In our blue jeans we climb over hillsides green from rain, with each step giving back to the earth crumbling mortar and bricks. We stand guard over a fleet of ocean-weary Toyotas. Discarded warships lurk upstream in a gray gaggle. Speaking of geese, they are forming, re-forming overhead.

We return to the cemetery, read the seating chart for the men laid out in rows, militarily anonymous. The dog soldiers give us hope. Their tombstones sit up and speak their names: Muggsy, Tuffy, and Duke. The new year is beginning. We call out our names from the Straits of Carquinez. We are still very much alive.

The Novel Begins Here

Sylvia decides to rewrite her journal,
beginning with the significant events
of a particular day in November she wishes to hide,
and asks herself if future scholars
will debate the differences in penmanship
from day to day, or lament the layer that is lost,
that shows up around the corners, fast-fading palimpsest,
and wonder which is the correct version,
for now there is reference only to the last
pomegranate clinging after all the leaves are gone,
a mile-and-a-half race on the turf, the favorite scratched,
footprints across the frosty grass, turning brown,
airline tickets received, destination left blank,
an ordinary day again, winter setting in.

Close Your Eyes to See

She leans against the door, pressing it shut.
Something about her brother, forgotten, papers in the trunk.
No war or madness brought down his plane,
or thoughts of climbing, for once, too high.

This is not a real attic, and she has been here before.
Fire enters the window—for an instant, blinds her.
She wants to invent a life he could have lived,
a story they can repeat, that they both know.
The idea she holds of him was his gift to her,
and it is whole even when the body lies broken.

Where the Words Are

When the day stops speaking
and my head empties, dropping into sleep,
the mice begin in the attic
delivering all the messages
I could not finish during the day.

And in the scurrying, bits of text
drift into my dreams, so seamless
the transfer of information
that I wake unknowing, surprised
at the ideas I have uncovered in the night.

Shall we call it, then, the walk in the garden?

CONRAD AIKEN
from "The Walk in the Garden"

Listening for Beauty

Europa, Remembering Zeus

Some might call it rape, the way he carted her away.
One moment she's sitting in a pre-European cafe, waking
from a dream of continents pulling her from side to side.

On the table a Mason jar of crocuses and hyacinth.

Handsome as a bull, he presents himself as eligible,
presumably an unmarried man. Hera must have
been out shopping, somehow he's gotten clean away.

Sitting with his newest flame, he traces on the tabletop
all the countries on the continent they might visit in a day.
Afraid to look him in the eye but somehow willing,

Sign me up, she says, and climbs aboard.

I don't think they'd call it rape, the years she spent
with him in Crete, all those sons she bore him,
water splashing all around them in their island dream.

The cafe owner missed her, once had offered her a job,
imagined presiding godlike over her as she knelt to scrub the floor.

Years later he received a postcard, *My son Minos*, she said, *is king.*

Le Bal à Bougival, by Renoir

Is she more noticeable in his arms, or more forgotten?
We do not see his eyes beneath his straw hat,
   but we know they burn.

The red trim on her white dress excites him,
his hand wants to slide from its grasp on her waist.

They are hardly moving but their steps are powerful,
he leads her even as they stand still.

All the while she watches the watchers,
knowing they are seen as lovers,
as invisible as a couple, but worth a few stares.

He is my sister's husband,
she is laughing over there beneath the trees,
and does not suspect us as the others do,
strangers throwing us a strange eye.

We are full of cold beer, caught up in the dance,
and the way he holds me I am staggering.

My left arm thrown over his neck
leaves my right side open.
This is something he knows well:
not to press too hard or smother,
but to leave part of the body untended, waiting.

Sex Is the Mathematics Urge Sublimated

Our impression of the saints is that they are rigid,
but a real saint knows the erect state opens
new channels of conductivity in the spine,
so that light and air, bearing the right message,
may rise in the body.

In paintings the saints stand as if their bodies
were arranged inside cardboard cylinders,
and when the signal was given their cover was lifted.
The mathematical impossibility of perfect posture
allows the saint no moment to relent,
except when not on view, for the saint is allowed
fifteen minutes upon waking before the curtains are raised.

The mathematician works hard to unravel
the secrets of perfection: draws with a light pencil
the position of the vertebrae. Her lover
waits for her to arrive at a conclusion.
When her attempts at saintliness end, he will begin.

Fielding

I stand in the center of a field of grass,
nothing happens for a long time.
I do not notice when you come to bat,
you are so far away and the sky is marvelous.

You used to tell people how I could
catch any number of balls thrown my way,
when it was quiet you could hear them
falling fast in my glove.

At that distance you look like any man in a white uniform.
I am drawn to them all,
a string pulls me toward home plate
before I know what I am doing.

My fist beats my glove like rain,
first hard and then soft.
There is no one to talk to out here,
we are all playing our own positions.

This time it will be different,
only you can hit the ball this way.
For me it is the message that never arrives,
I wave my arms so it will know where I am.

If I catch you
the afternoon will never end,
but the game will be over,
for you are soft and sit in my palm.

Lucia

Someone told her the center of the eye is called Iris,
goddess of the rainbow, messenger, fleur-de-lys.
No one mentioned to her what the eyes could do:
summon a man, cast a spell, capture light.

The man she captured would not let her go,
and she found him wanting,
found him less beautiful than God, in her eyes,
and she trusted her eyes to tell her the truth,
even though they had given her away.
Turning from his grasp she reached into a wooden chest,
selected her finest blue platter,
ran her fingers over its glazed surface
just before she made him a present of what he desired.
Take these, sir, my wretched, beautiful eyes,
and let me alone to marry God.

The blind follow the blind to Syracuse,
seize the hem of her statue,
work their way up to her hands,
the outstretched plate,
hoping to touch her eyes and see.

Death by Desire

Madame Bovary is dead, is dead.
Each night she wakes from the dead,
runs across grassy fields to her lover's house,
there are so many rooms we do not know
how she finds him. *Rodolphe*, she calls out,
his name growing longer with each breath.

She has planned their escape,
has ordered a full, lined cloak and a three-foot trunk,
but when he tells her the passports are ready, he is lying.

Go home, Madame Bovary,
your daughter is cooing, your daughter is crying.

The man you love will not save you.
The man who loves you will not save you.
The men who lust after you, even, will not save you.
The neighbors are peering through windows
and the priest is ready to cover your bones.

There is no life for you here
and no one to take you away.
You are more real than Flaubert has imagined.

The Concert, by Vermeer

Imagine the man who stole this painting.
He sees himself seated between the two women,
his face averted, safely hidden:
the woman to his right, older, his wife;
the woman at the keyboard, younger, not his wife.
The painting reminds him of possibilities,
the three of them seated there,
no sound but music,
fragile notes emboldened by the tile floor,
and then no sound.

Thieves have paraded this canvas past the helpless guards,
past the ghost of Isabella Stewart Gardner
and the ghost of her dog, who did not bark.
Each day the new owner takes the painting from his vault.
He is learning about provenance, and theft,
how holding is not owning,
how no peace comes with power.
He hears fingers pressing the keys trying to sustain each note
past time, past the limits of memory.
When he presses one of the women close,
time passes and is gone.

The Gift

She has brought pictures to him in the night,
without his seeing.
Intent like a thief she anchors the corners,
smoothes the edges with her painterly fingers,
arranges them one by one on her side of the glass
so that when he wakes up
he will see the dawn through her eyes,
ice blue and a band of saffron over rooftops,
the view from her window
that he has never seen, at dawn.

The woman he loves has summoned him,
his first thought,
so deft are the brushstrokes outlining the houses
he recognizes the view, and remembers
the many times he thought of staying,
buried in snowdrifts and winter dreams.
But she has not asked this of him,
he has watched her unravelling the ties binding them,
he feels certain the pictures are meant
to give him, in fact, permission not to come.

At Fourteen, Knowing Nothing

Beauty, she was told, must have something to do with sex,
something about the way the parts would fit together,
or were expected to fit together,
always, for her, the last thing on her mind.
Wouldn't someone tell her, instead,
about the stairs leading down to the river,
where blackbirds dance and children scramble,
learning to count each step in Spanish,
the icy water carrying bits of earth to their new home,
where a boat rocks incessantly,
a cradle, she thinks, we might make for ourselves,
under blankets, lying still, counting to a hundred,
feeling the tug of the line reeling us in,
cincuenta y uno, cincuenta y dos, the rope
sliding, our boat wanting to drift,
noventa y uno, noventa y dos,
and for the one who would tell her this story
she would wait
snug beside the river
listening for beauty,
whatever it was,
something to do with sex,
ciento uno,
ciento dos.

Scenes from the Garage

I am learning to speak like a man,
take my car to the garage and say:
the engine oscillates at forty miles per hour
because they will not understand if I tell them
the motor emits a low moan
that varies in intensity like wind on the moors.
But oscillation somehow relates to moaning,
from *oscillum*, diminutive of *os*, mouth,
meaning small mouth, the one
on the mask of Bacchus that hung
from the pine tree and swung in the breeze,
hence something that moves
up and down, or back and forth,
this movement centered on the mouth,
mouth to mouth riding the waves,
ohhhh, it begins, opening wider.
At the garage they pop the hood,
rev it up, they say,
and I sit there,
ready for anything,
surprised they have to ask.

Chillida-Leku

We wanted to call the photograph *Mammogram I* because
of the way the arms of the sculpture pressed against me,

and I thought of the women who lie back on their towels
exposing their upper bodies, bared breasts against the sun,

something I finally mastered at Bois Plage, ripping my
T-shirt off, but putting it on again when I heard the laughter

of small children nearby, and strode down instead
to find a swimming hole among the tide pools,

started to ask a couple who had been wading there
but of course the man had no clothes on, so he sank down

quickly in a small basin of water that barely covered him,
the way I tried to hide from the maid you had summoned

to fix the telephone in our hotel room in Hampstead—
but back to the mammogram, they sometimes have to do

one over, something about the tissues not lining up right,
even galettes are best flipped over once, seared brown

on each side, the Gruyère inside melting into the ratatouille,
butter brown, the color my breasts would be if the children

had disappeared, if the maid had not come to the door,
if the man had worn a swimsuit, if the arms

of the sculpture at Chillida-Leku, measured with a compass,
opened wider to admit all of me, facing front, exposed.

Marina di Campo, Elba

I wear the sea like a skirt, it is a prize I have won
for walking out this far. Fishing boats anchor the hem
where it meets the early morning sky.

Last night I met a man I could not believe in.
He fed us baked cod and cheese and wine like apples,
but what he wanted most, he said, was to touch my hair.

We told him we were engaged, *fidanzati*, we said,
and rolled laughing in the wet sand to make this clear.
We were not serious, not like this man,
whose eyes followed us from the dark pines.

This morning the fishermen have been out for hours,
and still I am the only one who wades,
and I think maybe I believe in this man,
like I believe in the sea, soft waves
surround me, wanting just to touch my hair.

Words, Words

For who can guess
what it means,
his hand upon your arm
(irrepressible sign of desire?),
for if he does not adore you
(sad imaginings of the moment),
he might be in need of a story,
any story from your lips will do,
but in the telling you cannot forget
his fingers insistent upon your arm,
your breath caught in an instant,
as the tree catches you
when you go by,
and it takes some time
before the story begins again,
and the point of contact is somehow
forgotten, as strong as it was,
stronger than all the close
mutterings whispered against
moist skin and secret places,
as if the hand upon your arm,
once all has been said between you,
was nothing but sunlight,
fluttering leaves,
the wind.

No sleep, not tonight. The window blazes.

ADAM ZAGAJEWSKI
from "Lullaby"

Shattering the Surface of Afternoon

Resting After the Fall

Where else would you settle down for a long rest
but in the folds of a hammock,
and if you were a mouse
you might find one, bunched up
like string in a large paper bag,
in the attic where you had come in from the hard winter,
tired at last from running between snowbanks and grain.

The man who had fallen out of the tree
rested beside her on the wide bed,
the attic window propped open to catch air,
and as afternoon drifted off
the image would come to her of the small, dead mouse
curled up in the bag with the hammock,
how perfect all its features were, skin on bones,
and how she had flung it a short way
into the berry vines and tangle behind the barn door,
the skeleton landing on rock,
the spine curved, motionless in sleep.

And as they rested together she thought
of the curve the man's body made as he fell,
the apple tree branch snapping beneath him,
dropping him like a heavy sack to the earth below,
and how she, rounding the corner,
was not in time to catch him,
and so held him now
all the more tightly in her arms.

What Was Left Behind

The water line after the pool was drained,
the brown stain in the coffee cup below the rim,
pink marks across the thigh, the panty line,
the place on the forehead where the hat was too tight,
where his thumbs had stroked her brow,
the suntan line, dark rose against marble,
the frosting just before it melted into the cake,
the residue, red crystals, left by the wine,
his hands on her hips, resting,
the palm prints on the glass table,
the calluses on his feet before she rubbed them with pumice,
wet lines on the pavement, how far the water sprayed,
strokes of the eraser on the page, red crumbles,
soft voices in the night after the lights went off,
the rattle of the motor, dying, after the key was turned,
the throat of the cello, strings still humming,
drops of sweat on her temples, the cool breeze,
her breath gasping in, in,
the long summer, its light dimming

Untitled

In the place in the brain that handles names—
Hannibal, Hannaleah, Atlee Hammacher—
the names are beginning to disappear, slowly.
Kissinger is still there, with Joyce Brothers and Idi Amin,
but my friends' relatives' names pop in and out
along with my sister-in-law's maiden name,
my sixth-grade teacher,
my first boss.
Some of my former lovers' last names are gone,
last time I checked all the first names were still there,
but no dates.
Fellows I went on dates with are also gone.
The room in the brain that keeps the names is airy,
breezy, the wind wanders through
ruffling the papers stacked on ancient card tables.
Use rocks, they say,
so I am looking for rocks to weight them down.
So nice to find you here, I know you—
perhaps I was once in love with you.

I have an idea:
we will be like Brando and Schneider,
we will do it without touching, without names.

Berkeley-Oakland Hills, October 1991

Fire takes the right-of-way down Tunnel Road
plays basketball with the firemen
leaps higher
throws a net over Grizzly Peak
catches slow squirrels in the lineup
lights eucalyptus candles for its birthday
eats three thousand homes
warms up for the '92 Games
learns to throw terrorist bombs
illuminates the page
never stops to reflect
waves to the city from above the hotel
sticks out its tongue for the cameras
laughs
erases the sun
embraces the lonely
ignites our dreams
grabs the fireman each morning

the rest of his life
he wakes up stamping

Holding Hands in a Dark Line:
Reporting from Tiananmen Square

She reads.
She pauses, waiting for the words to take effect.

The woman takes her place in a line of people, holding hands.
Her friends wave to her from across the square,
   their mouths open and close.

As she reads, a picture forms slowly in her mind.
The picture is forming even as she continues to read.
She focuses on the words as the picture comes into view.

In the act of reading, she waves to her friends across the square.
She reads the image of them falling, forms a picture in her mind
   of them falling, their mouths open and close.
She cannot tell you when the shots were fired.
She reads, waiting for the words in her mind to take effect.

Walking into the Future

What do you say to a man with a shotgun
when he is your husband
and has been drinking in the sin of your waywardness?

You tried to walk away from him,
urban walking you called it,
sometimes as far as three or four cities away.
You would nod to strangers who tipped their hats
and smile at the innocuousness of afternoon.

If the photographer captured you the moment you walked
into the kitchen, your heartbreakingly open
Netherlandish face would take it all in instantly.
You might gaze at the clock to register the hour of your death.
You would not ask for a glass of wine,
you would not want the taint of collusion.
You would not care about your dress, after the shot,
your blood seeping into the shape of France on your chest.

Mais où sont les neiges d'antan?
We used to repeat these words, the table between us,
two women mastering Villon.

Snow is what would be needed now to quench all this heat.
You are perhaps surprised to be walking away,
not flying like the other dead you have known,
but walking, light-footed,
there are sightings of you, daily, on the dusky avenues.

The Week That Abby Brought Us Spring
for A.N.

For who else could it have been, in the garden,
stroking the red-tipped rose leaves into bloom?

The moth cannot fly on overcast evenings.
Hidden from the stars, it stays close to the earth.

And so Gilda's voice glides over the lake of Mantua,
dying in her father's arms.

And just so, a lighted doorway hovers in the night air
beyond my window, momentary reflection, pointing the way.

We start over.
We look around us carefully and we start over.
We cannot remember a time so quiet.
We are afraid to fly, to glide on the lake.
We put one foot in the rocking boat
and wait for stars.

The Fires of Rouen

We who speak English have made mistakes in Rouen,
laying the city under siege,
setting the Maid of Orléans on fire,
her body arched against the stake,
and like a real saint
her heart did not burn,
so the English-speakers, to save themselves,
threw it into the Seine,
the heart still hissing from the flames.

And it was over the Seine
the British and American planes flew
in a single line, an axis of steel,
dropping fire on factories and shipping docks, and
because a few bombs were left or spilling out
at the wrong time, they slid as well into the spires
of St-Maclou, St-Ouen, and Notre Dame,
said the guide with a sly
smile to the Germans on tour,
and none for me, *persona non grata*,
American, church burner.

Rouen lives, *Vive Rouen*.

In one of the glass cases of the Hôtel-Dieu,
a mannequin stitched together by Madame du Coudray
showed her sister midwives
how to grasp the head and pull.

Upstairs in a room overlooking the garden
Flaubert was born, came down
the river looking for the world.

In the cloister of St Maclou, green grass
grows over the bones, and skeletons
carved into the timbers perform the dance of death.
After the war the windows of the churches
were unpacked and rehung, piece by piece.

All the places we look for Jeanne, she is gone.
The tower is washed of her blood and her cries,
the market sellers hawk cut flowers and souvenirs.
Beside the very spot a silver cross
and cement church soar upward mockingly
as if a plaque in the ground were not enough.

Her heart is in the river,
and just as we all began,
the river flows.

On the Way to the Bomb Shelter

I discover you,
whom I've waited for
all these years.
Your kisses disarm me,
say over and over
Let me introduce myself.
And there is no time
for the long, slow orgasm
of afternoon,
the shock of our bodies
is enough
to pull the trigger
in me,
in you,
and we roll on the concrete floor
spilling canned goods that travel
a long way before they stop.

Death freezes the egg in the skillet.
Death freezes the eggs in my body.

We open a can of caviar,
slide the salmon children down our throats
until I feel again eggs dropping inside me,
too many to be real.

Come, put your head in my lap,
dive once more
in the stream
you so lately discovered.
The missile that cruises above our heads
will not find us
if we are already
burning.

The Retablo

We squint to catch the action inside the glass:
a woman standing behind a counter,
miniature plates on the wall.
She is hoping to make a sale,
or she might be standing in her own kitchen,
a scene from the daily life.
In any case, she is surprised to find herself
in California on top of my dresser.

Our time in Arizona was brief.
The retablo did not come with complete instructions.
If she could hear us behind the glass
would she grant us something we desire?
We are flush with plates,
instead of pottery how about poetry?
The procedure could be the same.
We leave a few offerings, some
details from our lives,

like the photos and mementos
from our visit to the mission church.
They cover the effigy of San Javier del Bac,
who lies sweetly in an open case.
Someone has attached a Navy Seabees pin
to the hem of his robe.

I think of soldiers being shipped out.
The sky darkens over the mission.
As rain comes, we sit in our car
eating fry bread.
A dusting of sugar,
a prayer for the dead.

Madrileño

The man who had walked the streets
held a sign high in the Plaza Mayor:
Paz en Irak, bring our soldiers home.
This man would do anything for a change to come,
puts an extra packet of cheese, some bread, in his bag,
something to share with the strangers he will meet
along the way, in the same compartment,
walks with a spring in his step past the Prado Museum
on his way to Atocha,
takes out the ticket he has purchased to validate it,
a sharp, stabbing motion into the orange machine,
looks up at the board to read the track number,
smiles at the newspaper vendor. Could there be
a socialist victory? Not a chance, he thinks, only a dream.

Another man with a backpack passes him
on the way to the platform,
a man who doesn't smile, even as they almost collide.
He makes a mental note to find a more likely partner
for the slight meal he had planned to share.

The train arrives, one that will offer a comfortable seat
for him to dream in, arms to hold him,
peace in this world and the next.

Remembering in Part

The Church is auctioning off its precious artifacts.
My mother's hands press into the floured dough.

In lot three, a set of praying hands,
nineteenth century, Alsace-Lorraine.
With her hands behind my head like a benediction,
my mother pushes me off to school.

I am searching for a body, terra-cotta, to go with these hands.
When she danced with my father, my mother
had to reach up high to clasp his neck.

In the next millennium, all the severed limbs
and detached torsos will reassemble, will resemble a whole.
In a quiet corner of the house, my father holds my mother.
I find them this way, in my room, weeping.

S'io credesse che mia risposta fosse
a persona che mai tornasse al mondo, . . .

DANTE ALIGHIERI
from *Inferno* XXVII, 61–62

The Long Night of Flying

The Village of the Mermaids

We sit placid as wives
on straight-backed chairs
hoping to appear presentable.

Our blue-gray dresses drop to the floor
hiding the nonhuman parts of us,
tails that go thump in the night.

We have been told the men want to play with us.
We are shipshape, impenetrable,
no suck-holes to frighten them away.

We have spent time with our hair,
ridding each strand of reeds and mussel shells
until only the waves remind of the sea.

We cannot dance, or cook, or thread needles.
We weave nets rather than sew,
sing songs to sailors rather than speak.

The men see what they want in us:
fast women, like cars, sprouting tail fins,
on a jag, in a tailspin, taking them far.

In a daze by the side of the road
we renounce travel, sit like the women we are:
disembodied, deep thinkers, fool you all the time.

The Two Women

The woman who wanted to be talked to
sat across from the woman who wanted to dream,
and of course they talked about men,
the ones who flopped on their bellies
gasping for air along the dark riverbank.
And they talked about methods they could try to release them,
take them deep and burst to the surface still swimming,
how to stop the men from floundering.

Both women tried to imagine what the fish-men would say:
The woman who wanted to dream
heard a discourse on the properties of the line,
how habitats might be formed underwater,
layers of coral living and dying in harmonic succession.
The woman who wanted to be talked to
could not put words into the man's mouth,
but fed him green-lipped delicacies
and waited for him to sing to her,
round bubbly notes,
oh my love, what a hold you have upon me.

As the women told their stories
each wanted what the other described,
for a man who could talk about anything was better
than a man who wouldn't talk at all,
and a man who could sing would reach for her with his eyes.

Concord

In Sleepy Hollow, snow remains where there is shade.
The Transcendentalists rest in their slots high on the hill:
Henry David, Louisa May, Ralph Waldo, Bronson.
On clear nights they discuss the transmogrification of souls,
how treelike they've become, how settled into earth and stone.
They draw lots, decide who will drift down from the ridge
to check on the condition of the houses, the paint on shutters,
the ceiling beams, the state of the gardens,
the daily take from sales of Louisa's books,
the posters and pillows and *Little Women* dolls.
It is a refreshing change for them to look in on the mundane.
All the mysteries of death have been revealed to them.
There were some surprises, but most had gone according to plan.
They wonder if present-day visitors to the cemetery
pick up bits of conversation from the rocks and grasses,
all the best ideas there for the taking.
Sit still, they say, *like the stones.*
Imagine a place for your thoughts.
Imagine a place that is only thoughts.
Leave a trail of stones so you can find your way home.

A Short History of the Wool Industry

Reginald Conduit, wool merchant, Lord Mayor of London,
agreed in the eighth year of the reign of King Edward to raise
one thousand marks for soldiers to be sent to Scotland.

John Condit, weaver, got out of the wool business,
bought nineteen acres of upland, on the north side
of the mill brook bounded on Pisaick River East,
commonly known as Mill Brook Plain.

Jan Wynants, son of the painter, left home to take up
weaving in Brabant (where all the English wool was sent),
and in America helped to settle Elizabethtown,
named one of his daughters Elizabeth.

Peter Condit styled himself a clothier, put away
his father's loom, bequeathed to his "Loving Son Samuel
the Weavers Loom Commonly called Samuells Loom
with all ye Tackling belonging to it."

A twentieth-century genealogist will connect these families:
the Condits, the Winans, the Lyons, the Wards.
Computer software gathers up the names
once written in the family Bible.

Elizabeth Winans says to Ebenezer Lyon, when they are settled
down on a dark night, *I have a theory*, she says, *that every family
has at least one weaver. Or a wool merchant. Or a sheep farmer.*

Ebenezer is fast asleep. Peter outfits all his sons
in lovely wool suits: Samuel and Peter and John,
Nathaniel and Philip and Isaac. As young boys,
they run down to the banks of the Passaic.

I praise God and ever shall. It is the sheep hath paid for all.

Traveling Light

The man with the hat smiled
at the blue-gray woman, sometimes
told her what she wanted to hear,
or fell to moving clouds across the sky,
heavy armloads of not-quite-falling water,
clearing spaces between them in the air.

Let me take your hat, she said,
setting it down on a shifting cloud-table.
This is how delicate our contract,
the hat skillfully riding uncertain currents.

You might have thought her hair was gray
and her eyes blue, but it was
the other way around, or neither, merely
the effect she had on him when she smiled.

She couldn't decide if she liked him
better with or without the hat,
she could imagine making love to him
better without, but in her mind she would
see him nodding under the brim.

Now let's get this straight, he said,
we're here for a long time, gliding,
but if we push aside these clouds
we can see better where we were, below.

She wanted to look ahead, and said so,
saw mountains reaching out for the clouds,
embracing them in return for rain,
and the questions of where they were,
and where they would go, were left unanswered.

If he will only keep smiling,
if she will never let go of the hat.

Redwood Shores

Scat on the dike peppers the path to the oracle.
The stockholder reception has attracted
a pondful of Canada geese. Gray-blue heron,
in his stuffed shirt, inspects the hors d'oeuvres.
Sleek-swimming avocets, advocates
for the healthy life, stalk the high weeds.

The birds all have streets named for them
in the neighborhood, and appear as cameos
on the website for the San Francisco Bay Trail.
Pickleweed is spreading, latching onto a market.
The clapper rail is taking it on the chin,
no place to run, no place to hide.

The oracle has come to a conclusion: we are all endangered.
Warblers and shovelers will be circling the condos
on each slough, former home of, past habitat, no humanity here—
the weight of their endeavors has sunk a good lot of them.

Only a few natives left: the old librarian, the retired bureaucrat.
They search the web in civil twilight, sun already gone down.

The Unthinkable

I am worried about the act of flying
which I know I have to perfect
before I am lifted up.

I have tried to simulate the experience
by driving alone at six thousand feet.
I can watch the temperature gauges
like a pilot, terrified as usual,
pumping pedals when clouds come into view.

But if I am wrong about the flying part,
the mind, not the body, will take flight,
not Walter Benjamin but his briefcase,
not Leopold Bloom but the gray matter.

And do all the thoughts get to fly,
or just the ones that have already been discharged,
or maybe it is the other way around,
the ones already thought dissipate in the air
and the ones yet unbidden suddenly rise?

I cannot finish thinking about this,
and as for my unthought thoughts,
I bequeath them to you, whatever they may be,
for it is clear they will either rise with me
or if they are lucky they will go where I send them,
and you will not even notice you didn't think them yourself.

Interim

It was a comfort, after all,
to learn the dead were only sleeping,
still close at hand,
not slipping away,
and not only in dreams
would they appear, awake,
but on trains where we,
snapping to attention,
finally hear the conductor's voice—
Ma'am, where are you going,
and where did you get on?—
or when we wipe the glass clean,
startled to see a face not quite our own
and, beside ourselves, weeping,
awaken all the ghosts we can ever bear to see.

And every night we lie down with them,
practicing,
feeling ourselves slip away,
for what is the notion of self

and where is it tucked away
until morning?
Nothing of ourselves
but snips and snatches,
fits and starts,
the nap within the big sleep,
the dead telling us their dreams.

The Limits of Conversation

Bright-faced in the library stood my brother
as young as the day he left, forty-two years ago.
He had a new name, Piero di Brioni,
I saw it etched on the briefcase beside him.
There was a man with him, also Italian—strange
because my brother hadn't been Italian
when he left, none of us in the family were.
He asked if his car was still running,
the one, I guess, we found beside the airport,
really, I had to tell him, I had no idea.
He asked about my car but didn't know what an Audi was.
A cloud passed in front of his face
as if he knew there wasn't much time
and where was the conversation taking us.
You could be my older sister, finally he said.
I guess I am, it's my reward
for hanging around with the living so long.
I wish now I'd asked him where his plane had gone,
and what was in the briefcase, what was he selling
in heaven, and when I got there,
would there be some left for me?

The Movement of Beings

The wooden boats knock against each other in the bay.
This is the starting point for our conversation,
when we nudge each other, arm in arm.
We are walking up to St. Stephen's church, where
the ceiling is blue, the shape of an upturned boat.
The singers try not to jostle each other when they rise.
The lap and swell of the music washes over us.

When I was eighteen, in Florence,
I used to stop at Orsanmichele on the way into town.
In one of the niches, Thomas examines the body of Christ.
First you see the drapery: Verrocchio has mastered
all the folds and curves. But then you see the way
Thomas's foot slips off the front edge,
Christ drawing him into his circle,
Believe in me, he says to Thomas,
reach your hand here and put it into my side.

How do we learn to speak to each other?
During sleep when the heaviest thinking begins,
we roll and knock against each other,
nudge each other into dreams.
I dream you reach for me in the night.
You dream we are speaking the same language.
During the day we practice making doubt disappear.

Afternoon in Pienza

The ritual for parking is simple in Pienza.
You write your time of arrival on a piece of paper,
and leave it, visible, on the dash of your car.

You walk through the Porta al Prato, down
the Corso Rossellino to the main square,
perhaps the most perfectly designed in Italy.

On the right is the Palazzo Piccolomini,
home of the man who commissioned the square.
He was Pope Pius II at the time but
lived in the town as a little boy.

His books are in his library, you will read
them when you have more time.
The guard gives you a tour of the private
apartments of this most Renaissance man.

You take note of an astrolabe that appears
to be made of wood but is papier-mâché,
and a desk inlaid with stones whose size
and shape and markings make you see
a procession of black and white postcards.

You enter the church expecting it to be dark,
but here is where the Renaissance hits you:
Piccolomini had been reading Alberti, you see,
how the mind is transformed by the miracles of proportion.

Light from the windows buries itself in the stone,
turns its color from alabaster to rose,
a church where ideas can form in the head
and continue on to a measured conclusion.

You take a walk outside beside the walls.
As in most hill towns, you are perched
a suitable height above the valley floor.

Glimpses of green sing out in a bright voice.
The mind is free both inside and out.

San Michele

The vaporetto bumped against the island of the dead.
Gray sea against gray sky, ahead and behind her.
Now what, as she stepped onto the embankment.
Another one of mother's rules broken,
visiting yet another cemetery alone.
The vaporetto of the living made its speedy getaway.

Inside the gray envelope of afternoon
she could not see clearly, or wake the dead to ask.
So she unfolded the map she had prepared
and entered the cloister on the way to Ezra Pound.

She would travel back and forth
to the various plots she was seeking.
Her map had given her only a sketchy idea,
so she was not prepared for the hint of Brodsky,
a hand-lettered sign mentioning his late arrival.

She found Pound, and beside him Olga,
and Diaghilev, and a mystery woman named Sonia,
stretched out in a fetching dress
marking artfully her monument of stone.

Twice she traipsed back to the office of the dead,
but no one could leave to accompany her.
Brodsky's grave, they would have her understand,
was provisional, ah, that was why she could not find it.

The place they said to go
was overgrown with vines and weeds.
She stood where she imagined him to be,
a green lizard scurried by.

Tired from the ground she had covered, she reached
her hotel as the light was fading. Small heads
of women, muses perhaps, in terra-cotta, sprouted
from the sides of the windows in the courtyard below.

As the women smiled, she slipped into an envelope of sleep.
From the dead to the living, from the living to the dead.

Running the Bases

The first-base coach tells her to run on anything.
The third-base coach smiles, says, *how did you get here?*

The journey had been effortless
because she really did not remember running,
as if she had not paid attention to detail, again.

She dared not look back,
the runners were piling up behind her, one by one.
The opposing team members were eager to embrace her,
and she could feel herself tempted by comfort, and betrayal.

But her father and brother, standing outside the bases,
had guided her this far, and she felt nothing
like debt, or honor, only warmth, as if
the words and the smile were more than a gesture:
Listen to us, they said, *and you will be safe
no matter what happens, for you have learned
about the journey you will make to the riverside
where the boat is waiting, the arms around you,
the final letting go.*

*In this moment, look around you at this outfield,
this infield, write down what you remember
before you leave to come home.*

Intermission at the Scuola di San Rocco

We both had the right idea, picking up a mirror
to study the ceiling, looking down instead of up,
and because we were taking small steps, edging
toward the middle of the room, we might have
passed each other silently in the busy hall.

Earlier that day our train broke through the Euganean Hills,
an unlikely outcropping of hopeful green.
After they were gone the fields were flat again,
only so much work the Po could do.

If a gondola can be repaired, wood scraped and repainted,
and Tintoretto can remain fresh under close inspection
by handheld mirror, and hills can stand alone when all
adjoining land is fast asleep, then words can mend,
the hasty ones we wish to gather back again, all saved
by a look from you, from me, in the Scuola di San Rocco,
exchanging colors on our walk across the room.

Magic

Remember my bare feet
on the seat of the train,
a sign I made to you of
something more than friendship
just before the heron appeared
on this stretch of water,
as if out of the tunnel we were
made to see more clearly.
Think back on
all the looks I gave you,
label them exuberance,
or shyness, or flirtation,
then forget everything
you don't know or understand,
and I will speak to you plainly,
plant my feet
on solid ground near the estuary
as the train flies by
in its role as earthquake, *terremoto*,
shattering the surface of afternoon.
This is a real shakeup,
unexpected as the appearance
of bare feet on the seat of a train.

Look out the window if you can,
look for the blue heron
who waits for the afternoon train.

When he is not there I have gone home,
I have put on my shoes once more,
I am not there,
I have flown.

Clouds Brushed in Later

For the duration of a kiss
I enter your body willingly and drift
to the hiding place between your shoulders
where the angel waits, wishing to escape,
and where would we go without this
vision past white-curtained windows of blue sky
broken only by the appearance of birds
reeling from imagined height,
and as we glide together my long feathers
rest gently, fall back onto yours.
In morning the kiss that was a gift
has succumbed to a hundred sweeter ones,
and as if at the end of a journey
the window from which we first glimpsed
all the weight lifted from our earthly bodies
turns slowly on reluctant hinges,
presents us a last, momentary glance,
then closes with a prolonged click,
the curtains meeting again like lost friends,
and it is dark, our foreheads damp
from the effort of our long night of flying.

Notes

The epigraph for the section page "A Chorus of Pines" is excerpted from "A Tale," in *Selected Poems of Zbigniew Herbert*, edited and translated by Czeslaw Milosz and Peter Dale Scott, English translation copyright ©1968 by Czeslaw Milosz and Peter Scott. Reprinted by permission of HarperCollins Publishers.

On the section page "A Chorus of Pines," the photograph of a group of trees outside Arezzo was taken by the author in 1967.

"Bouilland": The ruins of the Abbaye Ste-Marguerite are located outside the village of Bouilland in Burgundy.

"Spinning": Virginia Woolf used to take walks in St. George's Gardens, a public park in Bloomsbury that formerly was a burial ground.

The epigraph for the section page "Listening for Beauty" is excerpted from "The Walk in the Garden" by Conrad Aiken. Reprinted by permission of Brandt and Hochman Literary Agents.

On the section page "Listening for Beauty," the photograph of the sculpture *Lo Profundo es el Aire XIV*, 1991, by Eduardo Chillida, was provided by the Museo Chillida-Leku, and reproduced by permission of Artists Rights Society (ARS), © 2006 Artists Rights Society (ARS), New York/VEGAP, Madrid.

"Sex Is the Mathematics Urge Sublimated" is a quotation ascribed to the mathematician M. C. Reed, according to Herb Caen (*San Francisco Chronicle*, April 10, 1989).

The epigraph for the section page "Shattering the Surface of Afternoon" is excerpted from "Lullaby," in *Canvas* by Adam Zagajewski, translated by Renata Gorczynski, Benjamin Ivry and C. K. Williams, copyright ©1991. Reprinted by permission of Farrar, Straus and Giroux.

On the section page "Shattering the Surface of Afternoon," the photograph of a family heirloom chair was taken by Riley Marangi.

The art on the section page "The Long Night of Flying" is *Evening Wind*, 1921, an etching (13¼ x 16 in. / 33.66 x 40.64 cm) by Edward Hopper (1882–1967), Josephine N. Hopper Bequest 70.1022, reproduced by permission of the Whitney Museum of American Art, New York. Photograph copyright © Whitney Museum of American Art, N.Y.

The Village of the Mermaids is the title of a painting by Paul Delvaux (1942).

"A Short History of the Wool Industry": The italicized line at the end of the poem is mentioned in Eileen Power's *The Wool Trade in English Medieval History* (1941) as a motto found engraved in the window of a wealthy wool merchant.

"Redwood Shores": Among the office buildings in the Redwood Shores section of Redwood City, California, is the headquarters of the software giant Oracle.

"Interim": The epigraph is excerpted from "Morning," in *Rimbaud: Complete Works, Selected Letters*, translated and edited by Wallace Fowlie, copyright © 1966. Reprinted by permission of the University of Chicago Press.

"Intermission at the Scuola di San Rocco": During the intermission at concerts in the Scuola di San Rocco in Venice, the guests are encouraged to ascend to the upper hall to see Tintoretto's paintings on the ceiling, and mirrors are supplied to aid the viewer.

Sharon Olson lives in Palo Alto, California, where she has been a reference librarian and cataloger at the Palo Alto City Library since 1978. She earned a B.A. in Art History from Stanford and attended its campus in Florence, Italy, in 1967. She also has an M.L.S. from U.C. Berkeley, and an M.A. in Comparative Literature from the University of Oregon. Her chapbook *Clouds Brushed in Later* was selected by Carolyn Forché as the winner of the first Abby Niebauer Memorial Chapbook award and was published by the San Jose Poetry Center Press in 1987. *The Long Night of Flying* is her first full-length collection of poems.

Sixteen Rivers Press is a shared-work nonprofit poetry collective dedicated to providing an alternative publishing avenue for San Francisco Bay Area poets. Founded in 1999 by seven writers, the press is named for the sixteen rivers that flow into San Francisco Bay.

San Joaquin · Fresno · Chowchilla · Merced · Tuolumne · Stanislaus · Calaveras · Bear
Mokelumne · Cosumnes · American · Yuba · Feather · Sacramento · Napa · Petaluma

Designer: Robert Perry
Printer: McNaughton & Gunn
Text type: Perpetua
Display type: Gill Sans Light